Wife Punishment i

rami zahra

Man in Islam is the head of the house, and his wife's reference regarding right and wrong. If the woman breaks the rules established by the man, the Qur'an gives the man the right to punish her, as it said to him: "And (as to) those on whose part you fear desertion, admonish them, and leave them alone in the beds and chastise them"[1].

Al-Noshouz "recalcitrance":

The verse called the breaking of the rules drawn by the man as "Noshouz". We read in " Lisan Al-Arab — the tongue of the Arabs": «The woman "nashazat "off her husband and on her husband tanshezo and tanshezo Nshouzan, she is a "Nashez": rose on him, was intractable to him, hated him and went out of obedience»[2] . Ibn Taymiyyah "has become one of the most influential medieval writers in contemporary Islam" defines "al-Nashuz" saying: "It is for her to shirk from her husband so that she does not obey him if he calls her to bed or goes out of his house without his permission, and so on. That is, any expression of self-fulfillment by the woman, whether at the sexual level, such as abstaining from meeting the sexual desires of the man, or at the behavioral level of refusing to submit to her husband's unjust orders such as staying at home, is seen from the angle of the verse as an act of disobedience, The husband must intervene to discipline his wife with the three punishment tools that the verse states:

Preaching- abandonment in the bed - beating.

Preaching

In the beginning, a man reminds the woman of his rights that were given to him by the sharia. He says to her, for example:

«fear God! For I have a right on you, and you have to decline from what you are doing, and know that my obedience is imposed upon you»[3]. " If she does not respond to preaching, the man moves to the second level of punishment.

Abandonment

The sayings of theologians vary on the second level of punishment (abandonment). We have the following statements about the meaning of the verse (and abandon them):

1. Abstaining from having sex with her, not talking to her[4];

2. Not speaking to her, although he can have sex[5], "because sex is his right.Ibn Abbas "He was one of Muhammad's

cousins and one of the early Qur'an scholars" said: "He abandons her with his tongue, and it is not pleasant to speak with her, nor leave her intercourse[6].

3. Restricting and raping her, a view chosen by al-Tabari "scholar, historian" in his interpretation. " To substantiate his interpretation[7], al-Tabari reviews the meaning of the word "abandonment."» in the Arabic lexicon, and refers to one of these meanings as: "abandonment of the camel, if tied by the owner by 'hijar', and the 'hijar' is a rope tied in the hands of the camel on one side[8]."Al-Tabari added: «The first of the correct sayings in this is to be (the statement of the verse) (and abandon them) referring to the meaning

of its connection to the 'hijar', as we mentioned from what the Arabs say about the camel if the owner tied it with a rope on what we described[9].

This interpretation is supported by a wide range of scholars, who have said that the meaning of «abandon them»«force them to have sexual intercourse with them and tie them up, from "hajr: tying" the camel if it is tied by the "hijar"[10]»..

Beating

The man should instill terror in the woman's soul, according to the

Muhammadi saying: "Hang your whip in a way that your family sees it."[11] An interpreter explains the rules of punishment:

« Light beatings, such as slapping, poking and the like which results in contempt and drop the sanctity, and with a whip, a soft rod, and so on, resulting in pain and suffering, and there is no harm from it, and no shedding of blood. If nothing comes from this, she is tied to the hijar, which is the rope, and forced to have sex with him, because that is his right. "[12].

When we analyze this definition, we find:

1. The beatings aim to destroy the dignity of women, and to inform them that they are inferior creatures without dignity

("contempt, dropping the sanctity»), in preparation for having full psychological control over her;

2. The aim of beatings is to rape ("and force her to have sex with him, because that is his right). Forcing women to have sex by beating was confirmed by Ibn Abbas, who said that a man has the right to continue beating his wife "until she obeys him in the bed"[13];

3. If the beating fails to force the wife to have sex, the husband ties his wife and rapes her.

4. We find in the definition the word "watea», Which is a common word in the language books and in the sources of jurisprudence, it is said: «Watea the

woman'means: having sex with her». «the "watea"[14] in origin means: to trample by foot. "setting foot on; stepping on; trampling down; treading on"

This expression reflects the society's conception of sex, where sexual practice is seen as an act in which a man tramples his wife's body. This word expresses the desires of violence and the tendency to achieve a sadistic satisfaction.

The Koranic verse does not specify the manner and limits of the beatings, but the interpreters say that Muhammad required that the beating should not be severe. . As this beating should be " light"[15], It can be:

1. Such as poking and the like[16];

2. Not beating on the face[17];

3. Not breaking any of her bones[18];

4. It is permissible for a man to use tools such as siwaak[19], "or" Shirak: the shoe band"[20], etc. .

A woman shall be beaten for every act that the husband dislikes or for any act that provokes his anger[21]. No one has the right to blame the husband for what he committed against his wife. Omar ibn al-Khattab "was one of the most powerful and influential Muslim caliphs in history" once hit his wife. When Omar was blamed for that, Mohammed said: "A man is not to be asked about why he hit his wife"[22]. On another occasion, Omar told a man that Muhammad said, "Do not ask the man why his wife was beaten [23]". So Abu Bakr "was a senior companion and — through his daughter Aisha the father-in-law of the Islamic prophet" did not say a word when his daughter Asma was beaten by her husband. She described her husband with the following words: "If Zubayr ibn al-'Awam "was a companion of Muhammad and a commander in the Rashidun army." was angry at one of us, he would beat her with a rod until he broke it[24]..Once, he got angry at her and at his other wife, and he "tied one's hair to the other and then beat them severely [25]". Once, Omar ibn al-Khattab came to Muhammad and told him that the

Muhajereen's wives became bolder in the city than they were in Mecca. Muhammad gave them permission to beat their wives. That night, many were beaten. Seventy women were said to have come to Muhammad's wives to complain about their husbands[26].

Modern and contemporary Islamic literature still value the beatings highly in resolving marital differences and look with satisfaction at its "educational results» , These are examples:

The first example is taken from "Tafseer Al-Manar: Al-Manar interpretation" by Mohammed Abdu, one of the pioneers of the Arab Renaissance (!):

« Some of the imitators of the Frankish in

their etiquette are surprised at our legitimization of the beating of women who are nashez. They do not denounce the fact that such a woman makes the man, who is the head of the house, subordinate, and despised, and insists on her disobedience, neither listening to his preaching nor caring for leaving her. I do not know how these women can be treated and what they advise their husbands to do with them (...). What corruption would occur on earth if a virtuous, pious man is allowed to depress the arrogance of a woman ... who increased her arrogance with a "Siwak" toothpick hitting her hand, or a slap to blow on her neck?. If it is difficult for them to allow this, let them know that their manners have become so thin that they have been cut off and that many of their arrogant Frankish masters are beating their women, the ludicrous and the naked women. This was done by their wise, their rulers, their teachers, their kings and their princes. It is an indispensable necessity in honoring those educated women. How can they deny that it is a necessity in a general religion for the Bedouin and the urban, of all human classes?[27].

The second example is taken from a contemporary writer quoting literally the words of the "Pioneer of Enlightenment": «Some Muslims who imitated the Franks may be surprised by the legitimacy of having a man beating his wife who is nashez, and are not surprised that this type of women rises up and makes a man, who is the head of the house, subordinate and despised, and insists on their Noshouz by not responding to his preaching and do not care about his abandonment, even though this might be hard for them. Let them know that the Frankish themselves are beating their wives, the polite, educated women, so did their wise men, their scholars, kings and rulers. It is an indispensable necessity in honoring those educated women. How can they deny that it is a necessity in a general religion for the Bedouin and the urban, of all human classes?. How to deny this since reasoning and instinct call to it, if the corrupt environment and manners prevail, and the man finds it inevitable, as the woman does not stop her Noshouz except by beating[28].

www.rawa.org

The third sample is taken from Mohamed Metwally Al-Sharawi, the greatest modern Egyptian scholar, who had a significant impact on the minds of Arab recipients:

"That beating is not a sign of hatred, but it may be a sign of love, and that as long as it is not severe It causes mild pain, and that man may resort to a light beating of the one he loves because he wants his/ her interest, and cares for him/her. Women, by their nature, understand this from their husbands, and know that their anger at them and punishing them fades away quickly and disappears after the disappearance of its causes, and they go on living together as if nothing happened[29]..

In the margin of the book: «Islam imprisoned», The author cites a quote by a Western psychologist called Hadfield. A.G. Let us read this quote attributed to this scholar:

"The instinct of obedience is sometimes strong, so that the person finds pleasure in having an authority imposed over him, therefore s/he endures pain happily, and this instinct is common among women... A wife of this type admires her husband more if he beats her and acts cruelly to her... Nothing grieves some women like the husband who is always kind, never rises up despite of being challenged by her"[30]..

The Islamic author does not mention the name of the source (the search or the book) from which quoted this statement, nor does he tell us about the name of the psychologist. We searched in "Google books ", and we did not find this name. Any way, we will not take into our account that this is a forgery done by the Islamic writer, and we will assume that the psychologist mentioned earlier is a real person, it is likely that he was dealing with the masochistic personality, however, the method the quotes were cited makes the reader think that the quotes state that the woman yearns for the man's punching, and that some women feel disappointed if the husband was «kind". And God forbid that the Muslim let his wife in her romantic yearnings.

Women As Sex Doll

Man in Islam has absolute sovereignty over his wife, and the relationship between them is the relationship of master and slave, as it was narrated in the hadith of Muhammad: "If I ordered anyone to prostrate to anyone, I would order the woman to prostrate to her husband"[31] ; A Muslim considers his woman to be a tool to satisfy his sexual desires, and he may impose this upon her whether she likes it or not. In all her situations: willing or unwilling, healthy or sick, her body is his. Had she been working on bread for the family, she must leave it and hurry to satisfy the instinct of the husband if she was called according to the Hadith of Muhammad. and here I state the hadiths confirming this[32]: "A woman has to allow her husband to have sex with her even when she is on a Qatab[33]" (Qatab: What is placed on the back of the camel) : "The husband has rights on the wife that if he wants to have sex with her while she is on camel's back, she should not prevent him.[34]"

- "Any woman who abandons her husband in bed at night is cursed by the angels until morning", on another occasion it is completed as: "Until she retreats and puts her hand in his hand."

"If a man calls his wife to bed and she

does not come, and he sleeps angry with her, she is cursed by the angels until morning comes"[35].

Those who look at the sources of interpretation and hadiths find dozens of hadiths in this regard.

Conclusion

The Muslim hears from childhood and in various occasions (in the mosque and the school and during his recitation of the Qur'an: (Preach them, abandon them, and beat them). This liturgical rite (preach, abandon, beat). This liturgical rite is a part of the Muslim's psychological structure. These tips become a part of his unconscious, and his treatment of women is based on his consciousness of the way he treats women, thus in the marital home she is dealt with not as an equal but as a slave for his lusts. Man has the right to possess her body and soul. In marital disputes, man has not only the upper word, but the upper hand, to beat whenever he wishes and for whatever reason he wishes, not to be asked "why did you beat your wife?" because he is the plaintiff, the judge and the executioner and he has authority over her; he has the freedom to do whatever he wants with her body. Forcing her to sex is not rape, but a legitimate right.

Fifteen centuries ago and on, Muslim women were subjected to psychological and physical persecution. The voice of the protest against the reality of women emerges dimly from women. Few have encroached some unjust rules, and fewer are those who came out demanding rights, and this tiny minority remains only barely heard because of the small number of claims for freedom compared to the broad female audience, who have not yet had the appropriate conditions to break the restrictions.

[1] Quran / An- Nisa 4:32
[2] Al Tafseer Al Kabeer, 3: 238, CF: Al Tabari: 6 / 696–697
[3] Al-Razi: 10/93
[4] Al-Tabari: 6/701 , Ibn Katheer : 4/25 , Provisions of Islam: 1/533
[5] Al-Tabari: 6/702
[6] Al-Tabari: 6/704, CF: Al- Qortobi : 6/284, Ad- Durr Al Manthour : 4/304

[7] Al- Qortobi : 6/285

[8] Al-Tabari: 6/705

[9] Al-Tabari: 6/707

[10] Al- Zamakhshari : 2/70

[11] Al- Zamakhshari : 2/70

[12] Al-Bahr Al Muheet : 3/252

[13] Al-Tabari: 6/709

[14] Lisan Al-Arab: The word Watea

[15] Al-Tabari: 6 / 709–710

[16] Al- Qortobi : 6/285

[17] Al-Tabari: 6/708

[18] Al-Tabari: 6/711

[19] Al-Tabari: 6 / 711–712

[20] Al- Tha'alebi 2/230

[21] Al- Qortobi : 6/286

[22] Al- Qortobi : 6/287, Ad- Durr Al Manthour : 4/406

[23] Ibn Katheer : 4/29

[24] Al- Zamakhshari : 2/7 1

[25] Al-Bahr Al muheet : 3/252, CF: Ibn Katheer : 4 / 27- 28, Provisions of Islam: 1/533

[26] Al- Razi : 10/93 , CF: Ibn Katheer : 4 / 27- 28

[27] Al-Manar 5 / 74–75

[28] Al Maragi : 5/29

[29] A l- Sharawi : 98

[30] Islam imprisoned: 237-margin: 29

[31] Al- Qortobi : 6/287, Rules of marriage: 70–71, Commandments: 97 & 98

[32] Ad- Durr Al Manthour : 4/406

[33] Al- Qortobi : 6/283

[34] Rules of marriage: 71

[35] Commandments: 100

Printed in Great Britain
by Amazon